Meet Author-Illustrator
Jennifer Owings Dewey

Jennif Owings Dewey

Dexter Elementary School
November 2002

Pai'sano, the Roadrunner

Jennifer Owings Dewey

PHOTOGRAPHS BY WYMAN MEINZER

THE MILLBROOK PRESS   BROOKFIELD, CONNECTICUT

PAiSANO, the RoAdrunner is dedicated to roadrunners everywhere, a brave, unlikely bird that never fails to give pleasure to those who see one speeding across desert ground.

All photographs by Wyman Meinzer with the exception of the following: © Paul A. Berquist, p. 7; © C. Allan Morgan, pp. 9, 36; © Rick and Nora Bowers, p. 15.

Library of Congress Cataloging-in-Publication Data
Dewey, Jennifer.
Paisano, the roadrunner / Jennifer Dewey; photographs by Wyman Meinzer.
p. cm.
Summary: The author describes her experiences with a family of roadrunners who come to live near her house.
ISBN 0-7613-1250-1 (lib. bdg.)
1. Roadrunner—Biography—Juvenile literature.
2. Human-animal relationships—Juvenile literature.
[1. Roadrunner. 2. Human-animal relationships.]
I. Meinzer, Wyman, ill. II. Title.
QL696.C83 D48 2002 598.7'4—dc21 2001044427

Published by The Millbrook Press, Inc.
2 Old New Milford Road
Brookfield, CT   06804
www.millbrookpress.com

Text copyright © 2002 by Jennifer Owings Dewey
Illustrations copyright © 2002 by Jennifer Owings Dewey
Photographs copyright © 2002 by Wyman Meinzer

Printed in Hong Kong

Contents

« A Legend From the Tohono O'odham People »

The roadrunner, Tadai, raced everywhere, this way
and that. He was looking for the edges of the Earth,
the shores of the oceans. He was trying to map the
world so the People would know their way around
and pick the best places to live.

›››› ›

Chapter One

Roadrunner Spring

The roadrunner was a blur at the edge of my vision. It dashed up the wall, head low, stubby wings pressed to its sides. Spindly legs with cream-colored scales moved under the bird like strings with toed feet dangling.

It stopped suddenly. Had there been tires at the end of its legs it would have made a screeching noise and reeked of burning rubber.

The bird stood sideways. I peered into a round eye with a yellow-gold center. A bright blue line traced the shape of the eye, and behind flashed a patch of red-orange. The rest of the head and face feathers were mottled shades of black, brown, and steel blue. The bird was gawky, but stately too, giving the impression of wisdom and silliness, sophistication and ragtag, a proud, well-dressed clown.

It turned its head, and our eyes met. The bird's every gesture, the way it stood boldly on the wall, seemed to say, "Whose yard is this, anyway?"

It was a cold March day of bright sunlight, the hour when restless winds spin over the ground from every compass point. Fingers of wind plucked at the bird's back feathers, lifting them as

if to glimpse what was hidden under-neath. The back feathers were brown and black, tipped with white. In the sunlight they shone with a greenish-purplish glow.

The long graceful tail feathers were a blend of pale olive green, brown, black, and bronze. The tips looked as if they had been dipped in white paint.

The roadrunner's tail twitched con-stantly, helping it stay balanced on the wall. Its stance, like its appearance, was contradictory: steady and uncertain, a cross between a cocky magpie and a nervous chicken.

"Where did you come from all of a sudden?" I whispered, sensing a shared curiosity in the way the bird met my gaze. "You are a nice surprise, and how handsome you are," I said.

The bird quivered, fluffed its back feathers, and blinked. I imagined a system of tightly coiled wires and springs inside its body. At any moment it would spin into a frenzy of activity, a dervish dance over the wall into the weeds.

Everyone knows roadrunners never stand still.

The roadrunner made a clacking noise with its beak, a sound like a train sliding along a track far away.

"Don't go," I urged. "Stay around. It's safe, I promise."

The bird might be scouting a nest site. It was the time of year for nest-building among roadrunners. In early spring the urge to mate and raise a family runs high.

The bird cooed, a low, soft murmur. I listened and wished I could translate the meaning of the sounds. Ravens have a language. Dolphins and humpbacks sing songs. Maybe roadrunners have a language all their own.

I studied the details of the bird's appearance as it stared at me. A fringe of spiky lashes grew around its eyelids, lavish and thick, lashes a human female would envy. By now it had been standing still for nearly four minutes.

The March wind, cold on my bare hands and face, swirled up and ruffled the roadrunner's breast feathers. Sunlight played over its body, shifting the hues, revealing luminescent greens, blues, and shiny blacks.

The bird spread its feet to steady itself in the wind. Its legs were bent sharply back at the knees. It scratched at the rough texture of the adobe wall with its toenails, making a sound like rubbing sandpaper.

Roadrunners are zygodactylous, meaning that they have paired toes. Two of the four toes on each foot face forward, and two face backward. Native Americans in the Southwest believe that the roadrunner outwits its enemies by leaving a track that goes in two directions at once.

I took a breath and slid my hands slowly down the handle of the rake I was holding. I hardly dared move for wanting to put the bird at ease.

It opened its tapered bill and panted once, twice, three times. Small explosions of air came with each gasp, delicate and quick, the sounds of a miniature bellows.

The bird suddenly sprang into action as if the coiled springs I'd imagined had tightened to the bursting point, the release of tension setting the bird in motion.

The roadrunner raised its short wings and leapt into the air a foot or two before swooping in a long, wavering glide to the ground, tail feathers spread like a fan. It landed at the edge of the pasture near the fruit trees and dove under a tangle of branches left to dry after last year's pruning.

The roadrunner came back the next day at the same hour—to the minute.

I knew it was the same bird, for I recognized the details of its feathering, the fearless yellow stare ringed with blue.

The bird came at the same hour four days running. The precision of its timing amazed me. I'd never imagined roadrunners obedient to a schedule.

On the fifth day the roadrunner's haunting calls came soothingly out of the brush under the apple trees. A second call came in response, from a new direction several yards beyond the first, the same whimpering coos.

chapter Two

A Family Affair

The new arrival looked and acted like a hen, which meant that the first bird must be a male. She was about twenty-two inches (fifty-six centimeters) long to his twenty-four (sixty-one centimeters), and she had no crest of feathers on her head. Her coloring was much the same, perhaps a little duller.

Both birds leaped to the top of the wall and faced each other. The hen bowed toward the male. He pressed his wings to his sides, cooing and lifting the crest of feathers on his head, gold eyes gleaming.

The male scraped his feet on the wall, repeating a series of coos over and over. The female turned her back to him. He left the wall with a bound, landing awkwardly in the grass. He nearly toppled over, but spread his wings to right himself.

In a graceless leap he was back on the wall, this time with a twig in his bill. He offered the gift to the female. She accepted.

The two passed gifts of stems and twigs back and forth, cooing a song of rhythmic responses for more than an hour. The transfer of the offerings settled something between them.

They mated out of sight in a tangle of underbrush, behind the wood pile, or beyond the chicken house.

〉〉〉〉

In the days following, the roadrunner pair came and went, traveling the same path through the yard, entering the front gate, darting across the yard, flying to the top of the wall, and leaping into the

«14»

apple orchard, stubby wings held wide. With each trip the birds carried nesting materials: twigs, chicken feathers, small discarded cartons from the side of the road, bark shed from cottonwood trees, and sticks.

I hesitated before looking for the nest, not wanting to disturb the pair as they were getting settled. When the rushing to and fro with nest materials stopped I went in search of their new home.

The pair had chosen a deep cranny in an old rock wall at the top of the orchard, sheltered by a line of tall cottonwood trees. The wall of weathered stones was low to the ground. Neglected for years, it was overgrown with sweet-pea vines and tangles of weeds.

Spiders lived in cracks, rodents housed themselves in larger nooks, lizards basked and scampered, beetles crept over warm rock surfaces, black and red ants crawled everywhere. It was an ideal spot, like nesting in a pantry supplied with all the food roadrunners like to eat.

I found a tree to climb, to spy on the roadrunner pair, the leafy branches thick enough to conceal me from view.

To get a comfortable "seat" on her nest the female backed in, working her way tail-first, her wings used like arms. Once secure, with her breast and a bit of head and bill showing, she half-closed her eyes and appeared to lapse into a trance.

The male scurried around adding bits of dried apple, stems, and dry leaves long fallen from the trees to the messy nest pile that was their new home. He poked and prodded, going about his work ignored by the hen, who clearly had other matters on her mind.

The eggs came over a period of days. There were six in all.

The female brooded chalky white eggs the size of lemons. For nineteen days she remained at her post, half-lidded eyes suggesting peace and contentment. I never saw her eat during this time, although she must have. I named her Edith.

I named the male Hamlet. He was wise, but a little disordered. Hamlet was often in the chicken yard stealing food, or zipping up and down the wall. We'd grown used to each other, in a neighborly way. One afternoon I decided to test how much closer I could get. I crawled across the ground from my spying-tree to the wall, moving slowly, pausing, working my way to within ten feet (three meters) of the nest. On my stomach, chin resting on the backs of my hands, I heard a faint tap-tap-tapping sound. Closing my eyes and concentrating, I detected faint peep-peep-peeps.

Edith ruffled her feathers, blinked, turned her face away from me, and adjusted herself over her brood.

I remained transfixed for hours, how many I can't remember, not wanting to miss the long-awaited moment: a glimpse of the first-hatched roadrunner chick.

Near sundown, when long shadows moved across the earth and darkness fell, a tiny head ruffled Edith's skirt of feathers.

It took two full weeks before five healthy chicks occupied the nest. The sixth egg never hatched.

Hamlet and Edith ignored me, so I observed the little ones closely. I saw their egg teeth, tiny prongs on the tips of their bills. They emerged featherless, naked black skin crinkled like old paper. Their eyes were dull brown, the insides of their mouths blotchy. Within days, though, they were dressed in long white hairs, down as fine as milkweed. The egg teeth disappeared. Their feet, two toes forward, two back, were oversized and grayish-blue.

The new chicks mewed like kittens and buzzed like baby rattlesnakes, fluttering weak wings and bobbing frail necks and heads. The biggest, first-hatched chick leaned against the others when both parents left the nest, providing warmth and comfort.

Roadrunners, like other birds, choose nest sites for two primary reasons. Concealment

«18»

is one, and food supply the other. In dry years roadrunners are infertile. Good rains mean a better food supply and inspire nesting. The birds, with their high metabolic rate, need to be able to find enough food to fill their bellies, and keep up with the demands of the young.

Roadrunners are part of the desert food chain, one that starts with grasses that create the habitats for insects, lizards, snakes, and rodents. Roadrunners eat these animals, and in turn coyotes, foxes, and ring-tail cats prey on roadrunners.

Eating breakfast outside one morning in early May, I turned, hearing Hamlet's clackity sounds close by. On impulse I tossed him a crust of toast. He took it and came nearer, snapping his bill, demanding more. I gave him more, and still he was not satisfied.

When the toast scraps were gone, Hamlet was off and running in the pasture. The next morning Hamlet came again looking for breakfast. Edith was with him.

"You've left your little ones unguarded," I scolded, giving each bird a freshly buttered slice of toast.

Toast became a morning ritual. I might forget or run late. The birds would remind me of my obligation, rapping and tapping at the door, clacking their bills.

One morning after toast Edith snapped a collared lizard's neck as if it were a toothpick. The lizard was basking, and Edith had come from behind, a surprise attack.

She stood gulping the animal head first. Slowly but surely, it vanished down her long throat. It was nearly an hour before the entire lizard was consumed.

After finishing the lizard, Edith stood on the wall and called out for all the world to hear, a loud clatter, like someone running a stick along the side of a wooden fence.

"*KaaaaaaaKaaaaaaKaaaaaa*," the bird reeled off her song.

In the distance, faint but sure, came Hamlet's answer, a chorus of coos.

Hearing this, Edith raised herself as high as she could, eyes wide. She looked loony and extremely pleased with herself.

Edith and Hamlet were feverish in pursuit of food, for both themselves and their babies. They darted up to the wall, eyes glazed with determination, into the back pasture, around the trees, capturing lizards, spiders, beetles, and mice.

The birds dashed low over the ground, bodies stretched flat, loosely hinged tails moving in every direction, balancing and

counterbalancing. They made sharp turns, zigging and zagging after prey. They dealt the death blow by slamming a lizard or other prey animal with a blow from their powerful bill.

The parent birds brought prey to the nest, dropping it to the mewing, buzzing chicks. If the prey was too large for the little ones to swallow, the parents ate it themselves and ran off for more, returning with grasshoppers, newborn snakes, baby horned lizards, and millipedes.

I spent hours under the cottonwood shade tree watching roadrunner antics, the rituals of roadrunner family life, not feared, hardly noticed.

Edith came from the ditch one day, her breast feathers puffed up like the bosom of an opera diva. She had soaked her body with water and carried the moisture to the

nest, droplets tucked into her chest feathers. She settled on her babies. Each one ran a bill across her bulging chest, dribbling water into their throats.

A neighbor, Mr. Lujan, came to talk one afternoon. He'd heard strange calls coming from my place.

"Got roadrunners?" he asked, using the shorthand speech common in the northern New Mexico valley where we lived.

"Yup, a pair and five babies," I said proudly, as if I'd laid the eggs myself.

"Good for boils," he said, scratching the stubble on his chin. "Good for itch, for tuberculosis, too."

"I know they bring good luck," I said, puzzled by what Mr. Lujan was saying. "How are they good for those other things? Boils and itches?"

"Cook up the meat," he said, eyeing me from the shade cast by his cowboy hat. "Eat the meat, drink the tea. That'll do it every time. My wife knows the recipe. Ask her sometime."

I nodded and quickly changed the subject.

Mr. Lujan walked out of the gate as Hamlet zipped in. The two faced off. Hamlet strutted like a rooster and raised his crest, cackling

«23»

and running for Mr. Lujan's legs. The old man backed away, driven from the yard by the guard bird.

I was proud of Hamlet, pleased that he took ownership of our place, putting his own scrawny neck at risk for the sake of protecting his territory.

Chapter Three

Fledglings on the Loose

In the first week of life the stringy white plumage on the chicks had hung sparse against their leathery black skins. True feathers, called blood quills, now appeared and promptly fell out. More came, fewer fell out, and the babies began to resemble true roadrunners.

The five remained in their nest, which grew ever messier and more disordered. They leaned half out when Hamlet or Edith appeared bearing something delicious like a speared vole, or a horned lizard.

Finally, the first young bird to hatch scrambled, head over tail, out of the nest. I named him Paisano, "man of the country," the common name for roadrunners where I live.

He was about four weeks old when he showed up one morning with his parents, wanting toast. Paisano had scraggly white underparts, grayish-brown back feathers, yellowish scales on his legs, and blue feet. He had an expression that could stop clocks. The look in his eye was pleading, sensitive, often alarmed, a poet's eyes. Watching him fresh out of the nest, staggering and teetering on gangly yellow legs, flightless and vulnerable, I whispered, "Oh, poor baby," as if he were a helpless waif.

Paisano and his four siblings were far from waifs. After they began wandering in the pasture, along the ditch, and in the orchard, their parents still fed them regularly, answering the demanding buzz that is the roadrunner call for food.

Paisano discovered the birdbath and took possession of it, scaring off intruders, even the magpies. Roadrunners bathe in dust or ashes, not water. They drown if they fall into rivers, streams, ponds, or stock tanks. Paisano liked the birdbath because he loved staring at his reflection. He was in love with himself.

I let him have his way at the birdbath. I spoiled him, and later his brothers and sisters, giving them as many pieces of toast as they wanted, and chunks of cheese and spoonfuls of scrambled eggs.

The roadrunner family came to the wall on hot midsummer days to cool off. Roadrunners have no sweat glands. To regulate their body temperatures they perch just above the ground, heads held high, fluttering their throats and panting.

I loved seeing them on the wall in a row, eyes half closed, tails twitching, even the smallest, the last to hatch, taking its rightful place with the others.

The family was on the wall one afternoon when I heard a familiar but unwelcome sound, the unmistakable buzz of a rattlesnake.

I rushed outside to see Edith facing off with a prairie rattlesnake sixteen inches (forty-one centimeters) long, coiled and ready to strike.

Roadrunners are sometimes called snakebirds. Folktales say a roadrunner will grab a cactus pad and beat a rattler to death with its spines.

This was not Edith's method.

Edith darted in circles around the snake, leaping into the air like a ballet dancer, twisting and turning, flapping her wings, creating a moving target difficult for the snake to zero in on.

The snake tried, lunging with its head, fangs ready to sink

into the roadrunner's flesh. Edith evaded each strike and continued her "dance" for several minutes.

The snake and the bird parried, as swordsmen do, striking and retreating, whirling about to keep track of what was happening on all sides.

Hamlet stood poised to plunge into the fray from his perch on the wall, his scrawny body shivering with anticipation.

Paisano and his siblings cowered and shook, turning their gazes aside as if viewing the battle was as risky as getting into it themselves.

Edith flapped her wings and screeched. I'd never heard such a sound. She struck at the snake, aiming for its neck. With lightning speed the snake's neck was in her bill and she thrashed the animal against the ground, beating it into submission, bashing it until its eyes began to bulge from its face.

The snake was still alive when Edith stopped beating it. In one move she dropped the snake and pierced its head with her beak, killing it. She took the limp body into her bill and began swallowing it head first.

The snake was too long for Edith to devour easily. It dangled from her bill for hours, until her insides were able to make room for it.

I worried about the chicks, who were at the bottom of the local pecking order. Magpies zoomed out of the trees to chase and annoy them, persisting with repeated attacks, wearing the little roadrunners out until they retreated to the nest to catch their breath.

On summer nights coyotes came into the orchard to pick fruit from the trees. Outside to watch the moon rise or set, I often saw these animals prowl through the grass, silent as wild cats, hungry for fresh roadrunner meat.

One night a chick was taken. I heard yips and howls, coyotes approaching, then silence, then an uproar of cackling, screeching, buzzing, and clucking equal to any I'd heard.

The chickens inside their wire enclosure added to the din, as if giving weight to the roadrunner protest.

None of the noisemaking saved the chick, the smallest one. It was devoured completely. Only a few feathers remained, discovered the next morning lying in the moist grass. It was as if the chick had run off in such a hurry, bits of its tail were left behind.

Chapter Four

Winter Blues, Spring Clutches

*H*amlet, Edith, Paisano, and the other three chicks were, by October, "immediate family." If I came home later than my usual hour at the end of the day, I was scolded. If I failed to present everyone with a "treat" both morning and evening, I was reminded with vocalizing I am sure Mr. Lujan, a quarter mile away, could hear as easily as I.

If the birdbath dried up, Paisano sat on the edge and squawked rudely, scaring the hens, alarming his parents, and bringing me running with a pail of water.

Hamlet and Edith, mostly Edith, still foraged for the chicks, although as the leaves fell from the cottonwoods in November the chicks were almost entirely on their own. They were moving ever farther away from their parental home, venturing into the fields across the road, down by the river, and into the dry hills beyond.

I wondered aloud to Edith one brisk fall day saying, "Edith, what do you think? Will any of your offspring stay around? I suppose you yourself don't know the answer to that one, do you?"

Edith gave me a sidelong glance, as she frequently did, blinking her lovely gold eyes and saying nothing.

Paisano was so tame he was more a pet than a wild creature. He followed me in and out of the house, tapping the screen-

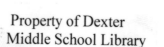

‹‹33››

door with his bill if I somehow managed to leave him behind. He even learned to open the door himself, sticking his bill into the crack between the house and the door frame.

On a day in late November it rained hard all afternoon, a cold, dense rain that soaked the earth and turned the leaves on the ground dark brown. The autumnal monsoons had arrived. Paisano came into the living room and sat by the fire, refusing to budge. I let him be, understanding that somehow I'd domesticated him.

For weeks Paisano was a "house bird," squatting in the kitchen by the stove for warmth, sitting in the big window in the front room looking out, rushing at the feet of visitors to make sure that whoever was coming was friendly.

Edith and Hamlet were truly wild. Hamlet vanished sometime around Christmas. Edith remained. She came and went, sometimes not showing up for several days. When she begged for food, I looked closely at her, to make sure she was surviving the harshness of the weather, not growing too skinny.

Once in a while one of the other youngsters would show up. Gradually they stopped coming and I knew I would never see them again. Hamlet, however, was another story.

In January a bitter storm blew in, rare for our part of the Southwest. It lasted three days. Snow fell as if it would continue forever, blanketing the country in layers of smooth white, broken by animal tracks. On the evening of the third day I heard a cackling noise. Immediately I recognized it as Hamlet's eager call.

Edith answered from somewhere in the gray gloom of the orchard. Paisano jumped up and ran for the door. The minute I opened it, he turned and darted back into the living room. Paisano was not one for being chilled.

Before it turned dark, Hamlet and Edith were at the back door begging. I fed them bread smeared with bacon grease, bananas, and boiled eggs. I figured nothing was too much for them in their effort to stay alive during the coldest time of the year.

Roadrunners are not known to mate for life, so Hamlet's attachment to Edith, if that was what brought him back around, was unusual. I decided there was a good chance that he was more attached to the food I offered. What counted was that they knew where to come when their stomachs were empty.

On days the sun was shining brightly, Edith, Hamlet, and Paisano sunned on the wall.

One morning a cat happened by. Paisano surprised us all by jumping down to greet the startled cat with puffed-up feathers and spread wings. Paisano did a little jig with his legs and feet, daring the cat to take another step.

The cat sat down and peered with amber eyes at the roadrunner dancing crazily in front of him. Watching, I wondered if cats had hidden strategies deep in their brains for moments such as this. To attack would be hopeless, with a confusing, constantly moving tormentor. To retreat would lack dignity.

The cat wisely chose retreat.

Paisano had won his point.

As March turned to April, I became aware that Hamlet and Edith were gathering materials for a nest. In the spy-tree I saw them busily coming and going as they had done the year before. They were not making a new nest, but were in a frenzy getting the old one back in shape.

The pair used bark, small trash items, sticks, and leaves for the main body of the nest. Edith got into the nest and tamped its bowl with her feet after lining it with cattail fuzz, feathers, and dried snakeskins.

I held back from going close to the nest in the first weeks, not wanting to intrude.

Paisano was not so polite. His upbringing had been confusing. He was not exactly a roadrunner, except that he was nothing *but* a roadrunner. He was fascinated by the behavior of his parents, and yet he was so attached to me I could not leave him out at night without hearing about it.

He pestered Edith and Hamlet for food, running after them—charging is more like it—his voice shrill and demanding.

He was acting like a bully, a rude adolescent.

Feeding him did no good. Annoyance motivated him, not hunger. Only after Hamlet turned on Paisano did the younger bird stop chasing. Hamlet dove and lunged at Paisano as if to inflict real harm, and that did the job.

Edith's spring clutch came to six eggs, the same number as the year before. Watching her brooding, her posture by now familiar, the half-asleep pose of a bird in a family way, I smiled with contentment.

When the hatching began, roughly eighteen days after the first egg had appeared, Paisano hung close by the nest, jittery and nervous. All six eggs hatched.

Edith tolerated Paisano's comings and goings, as long as the young male was not aggressive. He foraged and brought bits of prey to the nest, acting on instinct. I wondered, watching him nurture his little brother and sister chicks, if he might outgrow his domesticity and find a roadrunner mate.

Halfway through the summer Hamlet disappeared. I felt certain he had come to no good end, a coyote or a fox had taken him. Two weeks passed with no sign and I gave him up for dead. Paisano helped Edith keep the chicks fed with grasshoppers and lizards. If she'd been left alone perhaps half her clutch would have starved.

I held a ceremony for Hamlet, with candlelight and wishes for a speedy trip to the Promised Land. The Zuni people believe roadrunners guide dead souls to Heaven using their clever two-way tracks to fool bad spirits.

The new crop of roadrunners inspired more visits from Mr. Lujan. By this time he understood that I was not going to boil any of the birds living on my place. He took it in good humor, even when Paisano launched an attack on his boots and jabbed his legs with a powerful bill.

"Shoo, shoo," Mr. Lujan said, waving Paisano off. "*Amigo, amigo,*" he shouted, trying to get the bird's attention.

Paisano stopped attacking and stepped back. He stood still but for a twitching tail, cackling low in his throat.

"He's saying, 'How do you do,'" I lied.

Mr. Lujan smiled and backed away, waving good-bye.

There was nothing to do but accept Paisano for who and what he was, part roadrunner, part human. He did everything he could to assist Edith and her brood. He kept track of me. He watched himself for hours in the birdbath water, and when winter came around again, he took up his place by the fire, as faithful as any hound.

Afterword

Paisano lived with me for three years. During the spring of the fourth year he found a mate. Like Hamlet before him, he stood on the wall and cooed. He strutted, raised his crest of top-knot feathers, and scratched at the wall surface with oversized, gray-blue toes.

I named his mate Sally, after a childhood friend. They produced two broods in two years and then moved on. I like to think of Paisano finally living a pure roadrunner life, all road-runner.

Useful Facts

Names for Roadrunners ›››

Roadrunners (*Geococcyx californianus*) got their name from pioneers traveling west on dusty trails. The birds raced along by the wagons. Paisano ("fellow countryman" or "man of the country") is commonly used in Texas, New Mexico, and Arizona.

Other names are:

Bird of paradise

Chaparral cock

Cock of the desert

Corredor camino (runner of the road)

Faisan real (royal pheasant)

Lizard eater

Medicine bird

Snakebird

Roadrunner Environments >>>

Scrub desert, lowlands, creosote and mesquite flats, Upper and Lower Sonoran zones in California, New Mexico, Mexico, Colorado, Kansas, Texas, Utah, and Oklahoma are roadrunner habitats.

Roadrunners travel from altitudes of 5,000 to 7,500 feet (1,500 to 2,250 meters) and seldom leave chosen areas. They befriend humans and become regular visitors in backyards. Birds establish trails they never vary from.

Roadrunner Anatomy >>>

Adult roadrunners are about two feet (sixty-one centimeters) long, half of which is their tail, and weigh about a pound (under half a kilogram). The skin under their feathers is black. A layer of brownish down under their primary feathers enables them to endure snow, cold, and rain. A roadrunner uses its strong legs to run from danger. Only when it is stressed or startled does it take flight.

On cold days roadrunners sun themselves, exposing a featherless patch of skin on their backs, which absorbs heat from the sun.

Roadrunners make throat noises, and they rub or clap the upper and lower mandibles of their bills. Their bills are sharp, like scissors, and capable of snapping a snake or a scorpion in half.

Roadrunners live on a diet of moths, insects, spiders, beetles, lizards, baby rabbits, mice, bats, and snakes. They will turn over cakes of mud and eat the wood lice and worms underneath. In harsh times, roadrunners will eat carrion.

Roadrunner Behavior ›››

Roadrunners are loners except when mating and raising a family. Males stake out territory and call for a female, a series of coos that rise and fall. Males court a single female, offering her gifts of twigs or lizards. Nesting begins in March or April. The first fledgling to leave the nest might do so even as the last egg is hatching. Nesting materials are sticks, bark, leaves, snakeskins, and often, discarded human trash.

Females are assisted by males when rearing the chicks. Hens stay on the nest when approached, or they may slide over the side and limp away, distracting attention from the young.

Juveniles remain close to the nest for several weeks after fledging, begging their parents for food.

Folklore About Roadrunners ›››

A Mexican notion says that fried or boiled roadrunner meat cures various sicknesses. The Tarahumara Indians of the Sierra Madre believe that eating roadrunner meat makes a person run faster. In Mexico, roadrunners, not storks, are said to be responsible for bringing babies.

A Mexican legend says that once the roadrunner was a Royal Pheasant, but he made the Eagle King angry. The Eagle King declared that the roadrunner would never fly again, but would be stuck on the ground, an eater of beetles, snakes, tarantulas, and scorpions.

Native Americans view the roadrunner as a mythical figure with extraordinary powers. Tracks of the roadrunner appear in rock art and pottery designs thousands of years old. The Zuni people place roadrunner feathers in their moccasins to fool an enemy in pursuit.

INDEX